Introduction

In today's digital age, artificial intelligence (AI) is rapidly transforming the business landscape and companies that fail to incorporate AI into their operations risk falling behind the competition. With its ability to automate processes, analyze vast volumes of data, and provide valuable insights, AI is becoming an essential tool for businesses looking to improve their bottom line. In this context, "Winning with AI: The Key to Profitable Business in the Digital Age" is the ultimate guide to leveraging AI for business success. This book is aimed at business leaders, decision-makers, and entrepreneurs who want to harness the power of AI to drive profitability, increase efficiency, and achieve sustainable growth. Through this book, businesses can learn best practices, strategies and case studies, that will help them WIN with AI.

Table of contents

The Impact of AI on Businesses

- Automation and Streamlining
- Personalization
- Improved Decision Making
- Cost Savings
- Sales and Marketing

AI applications in business

- Sales and Marketing
- Supply Chain Management
- Financial Services
- Human Resources

Automation and Streamlining

Automation and streamlining are two of the most significant benefits of AI in the business world. These technologies allow businesses to automate repetitive and mundane tasks and streamline routine processes. By automating these tasks, businesses can increase productivity, reduce errors, and improve efficiency. However, the benefits of automation don't stop there. There are several other ways that AI is revolutionizing the way businesses operate.

One key benefit of automation is the ability to reduce errors. AI-powered systems can ensure that tasks are completed with the correct inputs and in the correct order, eliminating the risk of human error. This can reduce wasted time and materials, as well as prevent costly mistakes. By freeing up employees' time from repetitive tasks, they can now focus on more complex and meaningful work, improving overall job satisfaction and reducing the risk of burnout.Another significant benefit of automation and streamlining is the ability to speed up operational processes. By automating repetitive tasks, businesses can reduce the amount of time it takes to complete a process, resulting in faster turnaround times. This can be especially beneficial in industries where speed is critical, such as healthcare or manufacturing. Additionally, with the integration of AI-powered systems, businesses can identify operational inefficiencies, optimizing and improving workflows. This can lead to significant time and cost savings, as well as a more competitive position in the market.

Moreover, automation and streamlining are also essential in meeting customer expectations. By reducing the time it takes for products or services to be delivered, customers are more likely to be satisfied. They are also likely to become repeat customers, resulting in increased revenue for the business. A seamless and efficient customer experience is increasingly becoming a key differentiator between companies, and AI-powered systems help businesses achieve that.

The benefits of automation and streamlining go beyond just saving time and reducing errors. AI-powered systems allow businesses to operate more efficiently, improve the employee experience, and ultimately better meet customer expectations. By leveraging this technology, businesses can stay ahead of the competition, better serve their customers, and increase revenue.

Personalization

Personalization is a game-changer when it comes to building relationships with customers. With the exponential growth of data and increased technological capabilities, businesses have never been more equipped to offer personalized experiences that customers crave.

When it comes to ecommerce, customers have become accustomed to seeing recommendations based on their interests. They expect to receive personalized offers, tailored to their browsing history and purchase behavior. To meet these expectations, businesses are using AI-powered recommendation engines to deliver personalized offers and promotions. As a result, these businesses are better able to tap into consumer preferences and desires, which leads to increased loyalty and better sales.

In addition to recommendations, businesses are utilizing AI-powered chatbots and virtual assistants to provide personalized support to their customers, 24/7. These chatbots can simulate human-like interactions, understand customer tone and intent, and provide relevant recommendations and solutions. Whether it's a chatbot that assists customers in placing an order or a virtual assistant that helps them troubleshoot a problem, these AI-powered experiences offer convenience, speed and personalization that consumers crave.

Personalization is not limited to digital experiences. Personalization can also take on more physical forms. For example, AI-powered technologies are being used to create custom fashion products where the AI system considers factors like body shape, style preferences and color palates, resulting in a uniquely tailored piece for the customer.Personalization is not only about offering the right product recommendations or custom products, but also tailoring the entire purchasing experience. Personalized email marketing is an excellent way businesses can reach out to their customers with messages specifically tailored to their behavior and past purchase history. Personalization can also be delivered in-store, since businesses with physical locations can create unique experiences for customers based on their preferences and loyalty.

Personalization is a powerful tool businesses can use to augment customer experiences. AI-powered personalization adds value to customer interactions, increasing loyalty, Repeat Purchases, and positive word of mouth. By leveraging AI, businesses can offer personalized customer touchpoints at scale, which can result in impressive revenue growth, better customer experiences and a competitive advantage.

Improved Decision Making

One of the pivotal advantages of AI-powered decision making is its ability to process data quickly and with greater accuracy than humans. In a matter of minutes, AI systems can sift through vast quantities of data, identify patterns and trends, and provide valuable insights that would be impossible for human analysts to determine. This can enable businesses to stay ahead of the competition by making informed, data-driven decisions that are based on accurate and reliable information.

Another critical advantage of AI-powered decision making is the ability to reduce bias and subjectivity. In fields such as hiring, where personal preferences and biases can cloud judgment, AI tools can provide an objective and reliable assessment of job candidates, enabling companies to make informed hiring decisions based on objective data. Similarly, in product development, the use of AI can reduce personal biases in design decisions, resulting in more effective and better-targeted offerings.

The use of AI in decision making can lead to better risk management. By analyzing past trends and predicting future outcomes, AI can help companies make informed decisions that can mitigate risks and capitalize on opportunities. AI can also automate some decision-making processes, enabling senior executives to focus on more complex and strategic issues, while the AI system handles more routine tasks.

Finally, from a customer perspective, AI-powered decision making can enhance the overall customer experience. By analyzing individual customer behaviors and preferences, businesses can create more personalized offerings, thus increasing customer engagement and loyalty. AI can also help companies anticipate customer needs and proactively address them, providing an enhanced customer experience that leads to increased loyalty and repeat business.

In sum, AI-powered decision making is a game-changer for businesses, allowing them to leverage technology to process vast quantities of data, reduce biases and improve decision accuracy while improving the overall customer experience. As AI technologies continue to evolve, these benefits will only become more pronounced.

Cost Savings

AI is revolutionizing the way businesses manage costs. As organizations strive to remain competitive in today's ever-changing market, cost reduction has become a critical factor in achieving success. With the ability to automate tasks and identify inefficiencies, AI is providing businesses with solutions to reduce costs while still maintaining high levels of efficiency.

One of the primary areas where AI is demonstrating cost savings potential is in customer service. By leveraging AI chatbots and virtual assistants, businesses can automate routine customer inquiries, reducing the need for human customer service representatives. This not only reduces labor costs, but also improves customer service levels, as AI-powered chatbots can be available 24/7, responding to inquiries in real-time and providing swift resolutions to customer concerns.

AI can help reduce costs in supply chain management. By predicting demand patterns and managing inventory levels more effectively, businesses can avoid overstocking, minimizing costs associated with excess inventory. Additionally, AI can provide predictive maintenance capabilities to identify maintenance requirements earlier, enabling organizations to replace equipment before they fail entirely. This reduces the cost of repairs and mitigates any downtime or lost production.

When it comes to manufacturing, AI can help identify quality issues early in the production process, minimizing scrap and rework costs. AI can also identify opportunities for automation that can help streamline the manufacturing process, reducing labor costs and increasing efficiency.

Automating with AI can also create opportunities to improve product quality and drive down the cost of manufacturing, boosting ROI.

AI is proving to be a valuable tool for companies in reducing costs across various areas of operation. By automating routine tasks and identifying inefficiencies in processes, AI can help businesses to save money while maintaining or even improving overall operational effectiveness. Through streamlining operations, reducing labor costs, and enhancing customer service, AI can help companies remain competitive in today's fast-paced marketplace.

Sales and Marketing

AI has emerged as a game-changing technology for sales and marketing teams, providing businesses with powerful tools to optimize outreach, generate leads, and build stronger customer relationships. By leveraging AI-powered chatbots and virtual assistants, businesses can create a more personalized and engaging experience for customers that drives brand loyalty and promotes customer advocacy.

The ability of AI to process and analyze vast quantities of data quickly and accurately is a key advantage for businesses in sales and marketing. By using AI to analyze customer metrics such as click-through rates, open rates, and engagement rates, businesses can gain valuable insights into customer behavior and preferences. This allows marketers to create highly targeted campaigns that maximize the return on investment while providing customers with personalized experiences that improve engagement.

AI-powered chatbots and virtual assistants are revolutionizing the way businesses interact with their customers, creating more personalized and engaging experiences. By providing customers with real-time recommendations and support tailored to their individual preferences and needs, businesses can strengthen customer relationships and improve customer loyalty. This can drive customer advocacy, generating a consistent stream of positive reviews and referrals that can lead to sustained growth and profitability for the business.

With AI-equipped natural language processing (NLP) algorithms, businesses can analyze customer feedback and sentiment across multiple channels, from social media to product reviews and customer support interactions.

This allows businesses to stay informed of how their brand is perceived and actively respond to potential issues or opportunities in real-time. This can improve customer satisfaction levels, increase retention rates, and enhance the overall customer experience.

In addition, AI can facilitate lead generation and conversion, providing sales teams with insights into lead behavior and preferences. By identifying high-quality leads and prioritizing them for follow-ups, businesses can nurture leads with highly-targeted outreach that increases the likelihood of successful conversions.

AI-powered tools can also automate the lead nurturing process, sending personalized communications triggered by specific actions taken by the prospect, further improving the customer experience.

AI is transforming the way businesses approach sales and marketing, providing powerful tools to create more personalized, engaging experiences with customers. By analyzing vast quantities of data and providing insights into customer preferences and behavior, businesses can improve their marketing campaigns, generate better leads, and enhance customer engagement and loyalty. With the continued evolution of AI technologies, we can expect more sophisticated and efficient marketing solutions that will drive business growth and profitability.

AI applications in business

Sales and Marketing

Sales and marketing are two essential functions in business that can be transformed by the use of artificial intelligence (AI) technology. AI can optimize sales and marketing efforts by providing businesses with powerful tools to personalize customer experiences and improve targeting.

One of the primary applications of AI in sales and marketing is the use of chatbots and virtual assistants that can provide customers with real-time recommendations and support tailored to their individual preferences and needs. These AI-powered tools create a more engaging and interactive experience for customers, improving customer satisfaction, loyalty, and retention.

AI can also analyze customer behavior to provide valuable insights that help marketers create targeted campaigns that resonate with their target audience. By analyzing metrics such as click-through rates, open rates, and engagement rates, businesses can gain valuable insights into customer preferences, improving the chances of successful outcomes for marketing campaigns and maximizing their return on investment.

AI can analyze data from various sources, including social media, to identify opportunities for engagement with potential customers. By using AI analytics, businesses can gain insights into customer interests, needs, and behaviors, allowing them to create more personalized and targeted campaigns that appeal to their customers' preferences.

The use of AI in sales and marketing can revolutionize how businesses approach their customers.

By leveraging AI-powered chatbots and virtual assistants, companies can provide a personalized experience that improves customer engagement and satisfaction. AI analytics can also provide the insights needed to create more targeted and effective marketing campaigns, increasing ROI. As AI technology continues to evolve, we can expect further improvements in sales and marketing efficiency, enhancing customer experiences and driving stronger business growth.

Supply Chain Management

AI is transforming supply chain management by providing businesses with powerful tools that enable them to optimize their operations, operate more efficiently, and minimize waste. One of the primary applications of AI in supply chain management is the use of predictive analytics to forecast demand. By analyzing historical sales data, market trends, and other factors, businesses can use AI to predict future demand more accurately. This helps them to optimize their ordering processes, ensuring that they have sufficient inventory to meet demand without overstocking and incurring associated costs.

AI can be used to develop more effective supply chain routes, optimizing transportation and inventory management. AI algorithms can help businesses balance inventory levels along the supply chain ensuring that products are always available for customers while minimizing transportation and warehousing costs. This not only reduces costs but also improves delivery time, enhances customer satisfaction, and leads to increased customer loyalty.

Another significant benefit of AI in supply chain management is its ability to monitor the quality of products throughout the supply chain. AI-powered sensors and cameras can monitor product quality in real-time, identifying potential quality issues early on. This enables businesses to take action before any significant damage occurs, reducing the cost of defective products and minimizing waste.

AI can help businesses reduce the environmental

impact of their operations. By optimizing inventory levels,reducing waste and minimizing transportation costs, AI can help businesses reduce their carbon footprint. Additionally, businesses can use AI to manage energy consumption, identifying opportunities to reduce power usage and save money on energy bills.

Finally, AI can help businesses increase supply chain transparency and traceability, providing greater visibility into the movement of goods and materials. This enables businesses to track and trace goods from source to destination, facilitating better targeted recalls, managing risk, and making more informed decisions. Moreover, it also helps businesses ensure their suppliers meet ethical and environmental standards.

AI is a game-changing technology for

supply chain management. providing businesses with powerful tools to optimize their operations, reduce waste, improve throughput, and increase transparency. By using AI to forecast demand, optimize inventory levels, and monitor product quality, businesses can operate more efficiently and deliver better products and services to their customers. As AI technologies continue to evolve, we can expect even greater efficiencies and innovation in supply chain management that will drive significant improvements in business performance and customer satisfaction.

Financial Services

The financial services industry is experiencing a significant transformation through the use of AI technology. AI is proving to be a powerful tool for financial institutions to enhance their offerings and operations. AI can automate repetitive tasks such as loan approvals, underwriting, and trading, allowing financial institutions to increase efficiency and profitability.

A key application of AI in the financial services industry is fraud detection. Financial institutions generate vast amounts of data daily, making it challenging to detect fraudulent activities. AI technology is equipped to analyze these large data sets, enabling it to identify unusual and suspicious transactions. Furthermore, by using supervised and unsupervised machine learning algorithms,

AI can learn from past scenarios to recognize emerging types of fraud, providing the necessary protection for financial institutions and their customers.

AI can provide assistance in conducting accurate risk assessments through predictive analytics algorithms. By analyzing various data points, such as credit behavior and payment history, AI can calculate the probability of default to identify high-risk clients. This insight helps financial institutions to make informed and accurate loan decisions, reducing risks for the institution and its customers.

Another significant benefit of AI in financial services is the automation of customer-facing processes. AI-powered chatbots can provide customers with real-time assistance and support, increasing customer engagement and satisfaction. Additionally, AI-powered tools can help analyze data to provide personalized recommendations to customers for investment opportunities, wealth management, and other financial planning needs.

AI technology can help financial institutions manage their resources more efficiently. AI algorithms can optimize stock portfolios and trading strategies to avoid common investment pitfalls. This allows financial institutions to offer more competitive returns, thereby attracting and retaining a more extensive range of clients.

AI technology is revolutionizing the financial services industry and presents an opportunity for financial institutions to adopt cutting-edge technologies and applications. With AI's advanced capabilities, financial institutions can automate repetitive tasks, reduce the risk of fraud, make informed loan decisions, and enhance customer experience. The emergence of AI also presents a chance for the industry to rely on data-driven insights to make informed decisions, optimize resources, and remain competitive in the marketplace.

Human Resources

AI technology is transforming human resources (HR) by enabling businesses to streamline administrative tasks and automate repetitive processes. This allows HR personnel to focus on more strategic work that requires human intuition and creativity. AI-powered tools such as chatbots and virtual assistants can provide employees with real-time assistance and support, reducing the need for HR staff to answer repetitive queries and scheduling tasks. Moreover, AI can provide predictive insights to HR, enabling businesses to make data-driven decisions and improve employee engagement.

One of the significant benefits of AI in HR is the automation of repetitive tasks. Chatbots and virtual assistants can be programmed to answer frequently asked questions, such as employee benefits queries, with the use of natural language processing (NLP) algorithms. AI can also automate the process of screening CVs and resumes, making the screening process faster and more efficient. This can help simplify the recruitment process, saving HR personnel time, and resources while reducing the risk of human error.

AI can provide insights on employee performance through the use of analytics algorithms. By analyzing employee data, including performance reviews, training records, and time and attendance information, AI can identify the strengths and weaknesses of employees. This can help HR personnel make informed decisions regarding employee development and promotions. AI can also help businesses to improve employee engagement by tracking employee sentiment through surveys and feedback data.

AI can be used to predict employee turnover. By analyzing historical data such as performance metrics, salary, and employee demographics, AI can identify the factors that contribute to employee turnover. This can help HR personnel to develop retention strategies that target specific employees who are at high risk of leaving the company. These strategies could be in the form of targeted training, personalized career development plans, or incentives to stay.

AI can play a significant role in creating more diverse and inclusive workplaces. By eliminating the subjective biases from the recruitment process, AI can enable unbiased decision-making by evaluating candidates based on objective criteria. This can improve workforce diversity and reduce the risk of discriminatory hiring practices.

AI technology is transforming HR by enabling businesses to streamline administrative tasks and automate repetitive processes. With AI-powered tools such as chatbots and virtual assistants, HR personnel can provide real-time assistance to employees, reducing the time and resources required to handle administrative tasks. The use of AI analytics can also provide predictive insights to HR personnel, enabling businesses to make informed decisions and improve employee engagement and retention. Overall, AI presents a significant opportunity for HR to improve business operations, empower employees, and drive business growth.

Conclusion

Artificial Intelligence (AI) is transforming the business world, playing an increasingly important role in enabling businesses to automate processes, gain insights, make data-driven decisions, and achieve strategic goals. AI can drive profits, reduce costs, increase efficiency and productivity, and enhance customer satisfaction. One of the ways AI is changing the business world is through automation. AI-powered robots and tools can complete repetitive and mundane tasks, freeing up human resources to focus on creative and strategic work. This results in greater efficiency, productivity, and profits. AI-powered chatbots, virtual assistants, and customer service bots, are becoming essential for businesses who want to be available to their customers around the clock.

Another way AI is changing the business world is through improved decision-making and insights. AI-powered analytics help businesses to extract useful insights from vast amounts of data, making more informed decisions and gaining a competitive advantage. For example, the insights gathered from analyzing customer behavior data can be used to improve targeting and personalization of customer experiences.

AI also allows businesses to forecast customer needs and respond proactively. Chatbots, virtual assistants, and customer service bots can gather data from customers' previous interactions to offer relevant recommendations and personalized advice when they interact with them again.

AI is also becoming an essential tool for businesses looking to minimize risk. By analyzing data such as financial metrics, customer behavior, and market trends, AI-enabled risk management tools can identify potential problems early on, enabling businesses to take corrective action before the situation worsens.

In summary, AI is changing the business world in numerous ways by enabling businesses to automate processes, gain insights, improve decision-making, and enhance customer experiences. Implementing AI can enable businesses to meet their goals with unprecedented efficiency and profitability. To ensure they remain competitive, businesses must embrace AI as part of their digital transformation journey and be willing to leverage its benefits

www.ingramcontent.com/pod-product-compliance
Lightning Source LLC
Chambersburg PA
CBHW072236230526
45466CB00024B/2069